CHURCH DOWN THE STREET

FAITH LOUD

THE CHURCH DOWN THE STREET:
THE CHURCH WITH THE DUNK TANK IN THE SANCTUARY

An overview of churches that practice only believer's baptism and congregational government, with a brief comparison to the Cumberland Presbyterian Church.

THE CHURCH DOWN THE STREET:
THE CHURCH WITH THE RED FLAMES ON THEIR SIGN

An overview of the Methodist family of churches, with a brief comparison to the Cumberland Presbyterian Church.

THE CHURCH DOWN THE STREET:
THE CHURCH KNOWN AS THE "FROZEN CHOSEN"

An overview of the Presbyterian family of churches, with a brief comparison to the Cumberland Presbyterian Church.

THE CHURCH DOWN THE STREET:
IS THAT CHURCH DOWN THE STREET CHRISTIAN?

An overview of worshiping communities whose Christianity is often questioned, and their compatibility with Cumberland Presbyterianism.

Discipleship Ministry Team
Ministry Council
Cumberland Presbyterian Church

March 2016

8207 Traditional Place
Cordova (Memphis), Tennessee 38016

MINISTRY COUNCIL
Cumberland Presbyterian Church

The Discipleship Ministry Team of the Ministry Council of the Cumberland Presbyterian Church is the successor organization to the Board of Christian Education of the Cumberland Presbyterian Church.

First Edition 2016

Published by The Discipleship Ministry Team, CPC
Memphis, Tennessee

ISBN-13: 13: 978-0692675618 (Discipleship Ministry Team, CPC)
ISBN-10: 0692675612

We want to hear from you. Please send your comments about this curriculum to the Discipleship Ministry Team at faithoutloud@cumberland.org

OUR UNITED OUTREACH
Made Possible In Part By Your Tithe To Our United Outreach

Funded, in part, by your contributions to Our United Outreach.

Cover Photo - Aerial of lower Queen Anne, 1962 by Seattle Municipal Archives
https://goo.gl/IDCm5u

FAITH OUT LOUD

THE CHURCH DOWN THE STREET:
THE CHURCH WITH THE DUNK TANK IN THE SANCTUARY

BY JAMIE ADAMS AND ANDY McCLUNG

SCRIPTURE
EPHESIANS 4:4-6,16

THEME
An overview of churches that practice only believer's baptism and congregational government, with a brief comparison to the Cumberland Presbyterian Church.

CONNECTING TO YOUR STUDENTS

Many congregations expect church-raised kids to make a profession of faith in their teens, if not before. Cumberland Presbyterians baptize infants of believing parents, trusting God to call those children to profess faith later in life; that profession of faith (which often happens in the teen years) is seen as the children claiming his/her earlier baptism.

We also baptize persons at the time of their profession of faith; but this is for persons not baptized as infants, either because they came from a faith tradition that does not baptize infants, or because they were not raised in a Christian home. What we don't do is re-baptize people at their professions of faith, if they were baptized as infants (see Confession of Faith 5.19).

Some of your students may have friends who attend churches where baptism and a profession of faith go hand-in-hand. This may cause such students to wonder about this practice, or even to be jealous of their friends' experiences.

This lesson deals only briefly with our theology behind baptism, because there's an entire Faith Out Loud lesson on our theology and practice of baptism, entitled "Baby Showers: Baptism in the C.P. Church."

EXPLAINING THE TOPIC

Your students may have been inside a church building that had a big tub, called a baptistery (BAP-tuh-stree), somewhere in the sanctuary. These are used for baptism done by immersion. In this lesson we'll briefly consider some churches that baptize by immersion. It's likely that such a church is down the street from yours.

Even in the most homogeneous denominations, there will be some differences in attitudes, beliefs, and practices from congregation to congregation. By necessity, then, this lesson speaks in generalities.

The Baptist church down the street could be from one of the many different kinds of Baptist denominations. You can't make a general statement about what any particular Baptist denomination believes, because (unlike us CPs) each Baptist congregation makes doctrinal and practical decisions for itself. There are no official denominational stances on anything, as each congregation is a "law unto itself." Several congregations will often agree on particular points of doctrine of practices of faith however. Baptist churches also differ from the CP Church in that each congregation can ordain whomever they wish. Some congregations require a formal education before ordaining someone, but some don't. Female Baptist clergy are rare.

Baptist churches have no sacraments. They consider baptism and communion as ordinances (religious rituals) in which the focus is on the people engaged in these rituals, rather than God actively working through them to bestow grace, as CPs believe. Baptism is seen both as symbolically putting one's old self to death to rise anew in Christ, as well as allowing God to wash away one's sins. Communion is only for remembering the sacrifice made by Jesus. For Baptists, any experience of God while doing these rituals depends on the person being aware of what they symbolize. For CPs, God is active in, and bestows grace through, these sacraments. Baptist congregations insist that persons be baptized by immersion before joining. Most also require re-baptism of persons baptized in other congregations. Because CPs focus on what God does in baptism, and believe that God does things right, we don't re-baptize anybody. (Ironically, the first Baptist congregation was begun in 1609, with members being baptized or re-baptized by pouring. Full immersion, which is so important to Baptists today, didn't begin until 1641.) Governmentally, Baptist congregations may have a group of leaders make some decisions, but the whole congregation votes on major decisions. This is called a congregational style of government.

The Church of Christ down the street is also congregational in government, and also practices only believer's baptism through immersion only. A board of male elders oversees the work of the congregation. There are no clergy in this system: preachers are those with the spiritual gift of preaching but do not have a higher office than the elders. All members are considered ministers; no one is called "reverend." A literal interpretation of the Bible is important, so much so, that they don't use musical instruments in worship—not because the Bible forbids it (the Old Testament does just the opposite, in fact), but because instruments are not mentioned as being used in worship anywhere in the New Testament.

In comparison, CPs believe that all Christians are called to minister within their vocations, and some are called to minister as their vocations. This latter group become clergy, or ordained ministers.

Perhaps the most interesting thing about the Church of Christ is that they believe theirs is the only true church. The basic idea is that the church began by Jesus' apostles fell away from its purpose and purity at some point. In the early 1800s, some folks rejected denominational names and creeds and restored the true church, which is now the Church of Christ.

The Christian Church (Disciples of Christ) down the street also grew out of the movement to discard denominations and restore the true church, but they don't say they're the only ones who got it right. They have male and female ordained clergy. They are congregational in government, but congregations are also officially connected through a General Assembly (GA). That Assembly, however, can't order congregations to do something as the Cumberland Presbyterian GA can through its presbyteries. The Disciples of Christ Church practices believer's only baptism by immersion.

The above churches say that the only doctrine or creed needed is the Bible and belief in Jesus Christ, thus they would disapprove of our Confession of Faith. They would also disapprove of our "Directory for Worship," which suggests some and dictates some elements for worship services.

Independent churches are congregations that have no connection to a larger body or denomination. They may have congregational government, the pastor may make all the decisions, or they may elect a board of leaders. In other words, they create their own rules, claiming accountability only to God. They may or may not use ancient creeds of the church.

They typically employ believer's only baptism and baptize by immersion, but may not be adamant about it.

In contrast to all of the above churches, we believe that each congregation is both spiritually and legally part of something bigger: a presbytery, a synod, the General Assembly. CPs have multiple levels of accountability and support for clergy and congregations. Congregationalists consider themselves accountable only to God, which translates into being accountable to what that particular congregation considers to be God's will. None of these things mean that your students (who presumably either attend or are members of a CP Church) should avoid being friends with, or engaging in Christian fellowship, occasionally worshiping with, or doing some ministry with friends and classmates who attend or are members of these other churches. It's important, however, that CP youth have a basic understanding of CP beliefs.

THEOLOGICAL UNDERPINNINGS
There are two primary theological concerns with the churches mentioned here. One concern is that they seem to have an attitude of, "We're the only ones doing baptism right." They don't accept other modes of baptism as valid. Many don't accept baptisms by immersion as valid if done in another denomination or even another congregation of their own denomination. They may not blatantly say either baptism is invalid, but by their practice of requiring rebaptism in their own congregation and by their mode alone, they are indeed stating—by practice, if not in words—that their way is the only right way.

The second concern is that the churches mentioned here probably hold the attitude that believer's baptism is the only valid baptism, because it's the only one specifically mentioned in the Bible. Holding scripture in high regard is a good thing to do, but these churches go too far. For them, it seems, God can't reveal God's will in any other way besides scripture, and God ceased revealing God's will when the Bible was completed. This attitude of, "We're the only ones doing baptism right" can and often does lead to the mindset of, "We're the only ones with the right theology." The Church of Christ even goes a step further to say they are the only true church.

The Cumberland Presbyterian Church never says we are the only Christians with the correct theology and practices. We do, however, say that our theology and practices are what's best for us. Every CP elder and minister has declared his/her adoption of, and promise to defend, that which distinguishes us as Cumberland Presbyterian: our Confession of Faith and Constitution (see Constitution 2.92 II and III, 3.63 II and III).

All forms of baptism practiced today probably developed within the church, rather than being exactly what we read in scripture. We acknowledge that; these others don't.

APPLYING THE LESSON TO YOUR OWN LIFE
On a scale of 1 (lowest) to 5 (highest), how well do you think the typical church member in the U.S. knows the theology of his/her church? How important do you think it is for a church member to know such things?

Using that same scale, how well do you think the typical member of your congregation knows Cumberland Presbyterian theology? How important do you think it is for CPs to know our theology?

How well do you know CP theology? What percentage of your beliefs about the theological issues mentioned in this lesson would you say comes from CP sources, and what percentage comes from other sources (readings, cultural osmosis, hymns, TV preachers, personal beliefs, etc.)? How does your congregation's session ensure that prospective members understand CP theology before joining? How does your session ensure members continue to expand their understanding of our theology?

Do you think the church having denominations saddens God, or does God want each believer in the denomination/church where he/she fits best?

THE CHURCH DOWN THE STREET:
THE CHURCH WITH THE DUNK TANK IN THE SANCTUARY

SCRIPTURE
EPHESIANS 4:4-6,16

RESOURCE LIST

LEADER PREP

- Bible
- Newsprint
- Painter's tape
- Large blank canvas or large poster board
- Markers, pens, paint

BEFORE THE LESSON

At the top of each page of newsprint, write one of the different denominations (including Cumberland Presbyterians mentioned in this lesson. Hang them around the room. As students enter the meeting place, invite them to write anything they know, or may think of, when they think about each denomination. These will be the springboard for the initial conversation. You might even make copies of this section for each student.

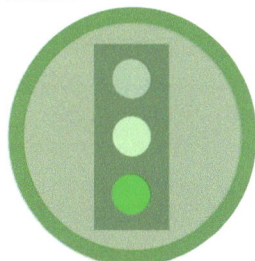

GET STARTED (10 minutes)

As students enter, ask them to write anything they know, or may think of when they think about each denomiantion listed around the room. After giving them time to arrive and respond, review what the students wrote about the different denominations listed on the newsprint.

On a separate piece of newsprint, collect and organize the responses. Fill in gaps for parallels where needed. For instance, if something was mentioned about baptism for one denomination, lead students in discussion about baptism at the others. Briefly discuss what they think about these differences, and why they think they might exist. Ask students to justify and explain their responses, if they can.

LISTEN UP (20 minutes)

ASK: How do you think churches developed into different denominations?

Allow students to speculate.

ASK: Do you think the differences between the denominations are significant?

DISCUSSION QUESTIONS

Some of the students may even be visiting from another church. Invite them to share the differences they observe. They may understand the theology behind the differences, but if not, supplement their sharing with the Leader Insight information on pages 5 and 6. It is okay if no one knows why some of the differences exist.

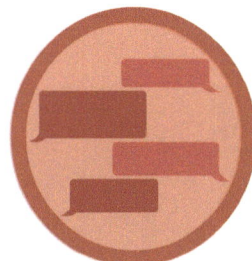

Review the histories and explanations of the different denominations in the Explaining the Topic section with the students. Make sure to highlight the differences in an objective way, so that one does not seem inferior to the others.

Have the students read Ephesians 4:4-6

[4] There is one body and one Spirit, just as you were called to one hope when you were called; [5] one Lord, one faith, one baptism; [6] one God and Father of all, who is over all and through all and in all.

ASK: What do you think Paul is saying here about unity?

ASK: If unity is so important, why do you think there are so many differences in churches?

DISCUSSION QUESTIONS

ASK: What do you think God thinks about all the different denominations?

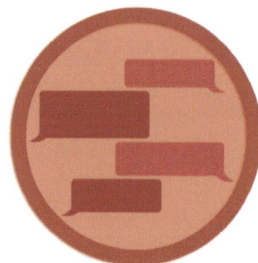

NOW WHAT? (15 minutes)
Read Ephesians 4:16
[16] From him the whole body, joined and held together by every supporting ligament, grows and builds itself up in love, as each part does its work.

NOW WHAT

ASK: What makes up the body he's talking about? (Guide answers towards the differences mentioned throughout this lesson.)

ASK: What are the "ligaments" that hold those parts together? (Answers should be along the lines of love, commitment, scripture, God, etc.)

ASK: Given your answers and this text, what is our responsibility as members of a CP church?

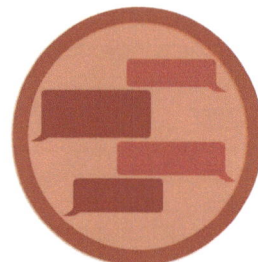

DISCUSSION QUESTIONS

ACTIVITY: A Loving Heart - on the canvas or poster board, draw a large heart (or circle, or hand; feel free to be creative here) covering the majority of the surface. Invite students to write things that all of the denominations talked about have in common. Perhaps they can also include ways that the churches from different denominations can serve together. When it is finished, hang it up in the meeting room or a prominent place as a reminder of how everyone is a valuable part of the body of the universal church.

LIVE IT

LIVE IT (5 minutes)

Challenge students to find ways to serve with their friends who may be from a different church denomination. Look for opportunities where they can work side by side despite their worshiping differences, perhaps in some form of community service.

CLOSE IN PRAYER: Most Holy God, thank you for all the church denominations in this community that, while outwardly seem very different, inside share in the belief that you alone are Lord and Savior. We're glad that you can use each of those churches and also each of us, in our uniqueness, to come together and be part of one amazing kingdom. Amen.

JUST IN CASE

While this lesson is not about baptism itself, one of your students may wish to discuss the topic. Christians argue about baptism a lot. Some of the non-CP churches mentioned here claim that believer's only baptism by immersion is the only form of baptism mentioned in scripture and is, therefore, the only right way to do it. Truthfully, though, we don't know how the early Church did baptisms. The description of Jesus' baptism in the gospels has no details, and in fact wasn't a Christian baptism. It was a Jewish cleansing ritual. Based on early Christian art work (A.D. 200-400), it's likely that the recipient of baptism stood or knelt in moving water and had water poured over his or her head. As for infant baptism, there are several Biblical passages with entire households being baptized upon a parent's conversion to Christianity. Surely some of those households had children in them, which would support the CP belief that parents can choose baptism for their children. Also, the Greek word used in the New Testament and translated as "to baptize" can mean either "to pour water over" or "to dip into water," depending on the context. The Biblical passages depicting baptism do not offer sufficient context to make a definitive conclusion. (Even when Matthew and Mark say Jesus came up out of the water, this could just as easily mean rising to his feet or climbing up the bank, as it could mean rising from being completely underwater.)

NOTES

Resources used in compiling background information: church-of-christ.org, disciples.org, Religions of America by Leo Rosten, ed., Westminster Dictionary of Theological Terms. Pictures used: 20150719_112425 by Brian Kelley - https://goo.gl/JLhVmN, 1950 Baptism - Pine Grove Baptist, October 22,1950 by Jill Carlson (jillcarlson.org) - https://goo.gl/9wAKYF, Baptism of Christ 11 by Waiting For The Word - https://goo.gl/13nfjO, Old Regular Baptist Church by Michael Carian - https://goo.gl/s5xQjE

FAITH OUT LOUD

THE CHURCH DOWN THE STREET:
THE CHURCH WITH THE RED FLAMES ON THEIR SIGN

BY JOANNA SIMMERMAN and ANDY McCLUNG

SCRIPTURE
JOHN 3:16, ACTS 2:1-3, 1 TIMOTHY 3:1-3

THEME
An overview of the Methodist family of churches, with a brief comparison to the Cumberland Presbyterian Church.

CONNECTING TO YOUR STUDENTS

For their entire lives, U.S. teens have heard from culture—both subtly and overtly—that all religions are the same, and that an individual's specific beliefs don't really matter, if he or she is sincere in them and tries to be a good person. (This is the overall message. They may occasionally hear that a specific religion is evil or wrong.) Most Christians would say, however, that salvation through Christ is more important than being sincere...or even religious.

Critics try to discredit Christianity by noting how many different denominations there are, and how many disagreements exist between them. But when folks think something is important, they get passionate about it; nobody passionately argues about things that aren't important.

If your students have visited other churches with friends or relatives, there's a good chance they've been in a Methodist church. If so, and depending on which type of Methodist church they visited, they may have come away wondering if there even are any differences between "us" and "them." There are, and they're significant.

EXPLAINING THE TOPIC

There are several denominations that carry the name "Methodist," more than we'll cover here. They all share roots in John Wesley, a priest in the Church of England (a.k.a. the Anglican Church), who was more enthusiastic about his faith than most Anglicans. During a period of professional burn out and personal depression, Wesley was at a Bible study in London (in 1738) when, as he says, "I felt my heart strangely warmed. I felt I did trust in Christ, Christ alone for salvation; and an assurance was given me that He had taken away my sins." This experience gave Wesley new energy in his ministry, particularly in his evangelistic preaching.

The African Methodist Episcopal Church (AME) is a predominantly African-American denomination with about 3.5 million members located in the U.S., the Caribbean, and Africa. Their motto is, "God Our Father, Christ Our Redeemer, the Holy Spirit Our Comforter, Humankind Our Family."

The African Methodist Episcopal Zion Church (AMEZ) is a predominantly African-American denomination with about 1.2 million members located in the U.S., the Caribbean, and Africa.

The Christian Methodist Episcopal (CME) is a predominantly African-American denomination with about 800,000 members in about 3,000 congregations located in the U.S., West Africa, Haiti, and Jamaica. Like the CP Church, this denomination was born in Tennessee. The first congregation (established in 1870, in Jackson, Tennessee, by a group of former slaves) is still there. It's called Mother Liberty.

The above three denominations share the theology and structure of the Methodist Church, from which they all separated at various points in American history. The division was not due to theological differences, but social differences. The founders of these denominations didn't think it was God's will for some humans to own others.

The church down the street from yours may be part of the United Methodist Church, the largest Methodist denomination in the US. Their logo is a skinny cross with red flame on the left side. This logo represents how humankind (and the United Methodist Church in particular) relates to God: through Jesus Christ. The single flame has two tongues. This harkens back to Pentecost, represents the presence of the Holy Spirit at work in and through the denomination, gives a nod to Wesley's heart-warming experience, and serves as a reminder that two denominations came together as one.

The "United" in the name comes from the uniting of two denominations in 1968: The Evangelical United Brethren Church (which itself was formed when two other denominations united in 1946) and The

Methodist Church (which itself was formed when three other denominations united in 1939). There are about 12 million members in the world, more than 7 million of them in the U.S. and the rest in Africa, Asia, and Europe. Membership is multi-racial.

The number of theological differences between most Methodist churches and the CP Church are few, but they are important points of disagreement (see below). The Methodist worship style is much the same as ours, but can vary significantly from congregation to congregation, just like ours. Some congregations pay close attention to the liturgical calendar, and some don't. Some congregations use paraments, and some don't.

Methodists, like us, recognize that each congregation is not its own authority, and the pastor is not the sole theological authority in a congregation. Like ours, every Methodist congregation is connected. Like us, no one person is in charge of the whole denomination. Like us, authority is shared by laity and clergy. A Methodist denomination will be structured in different levels, with each level having paid administrative staff. Those levels are described here from the top down. General Conference is the overarching body. It meets every four years. Annual Conference is geographic, meets annually, and is the "basic unit" of the church. An elected bishop serves over one or more Annual Conferences, and Annual Conferences elect an equal number of lay and clergy delegates to represent them at General Conference. Each Annual Conference is divided into geographically-determined districts. Each congregation is part of a district and is led by a church council of laypersons called the Staff Parish Relations Committee (SPRC). The paid administrator at the district level is a district superintendent. This type of church structure is called an Episcopal form of government, because it has bishops.

There are three forms of church government: congregational, episcopal, and presbyterian.

United Methodists have clergy of both genders. Bishops appoint clergy to, and remove them from, pastorates and other ministries. This is why it may seem like the Methodist church down the street changes pastors every couple of years. The session of a CP congregation, with presbytery's approval, calls whomever they wish to be their pastor, and under normal circumstances, that relationship between pastor and congregation remains intact until session or pastor asks presbytery to end it. Some United Methodist ministers are approved to preside over the sacraments only in the particular congregation to which they're appointed. CP clergy can preside over the sacraments anywhere.

Methodists baptize by sprinkling, pouring, or immersion. Like us, infant baptism is expected of churched families. Like us, communion is seen as symbolic; the bread and wine never change into anything else. The change is in us—a spiritual change brought about by God's grace, which flows through the sacrament. Baptism and communion are seen as sacraments (vehicles of God's grace) and are the only sacraments.

THEOLOGICAL UNDERPINNINGS
Methodists and CPs agree that God didn't predestine who is saved and who isn't. The two also agree that God acts first in salvation by extending grace. So, the person being saved is responding to God. In other words, we don't just suddenly decide, all on our own, to get saved. God calls us to salvation when the time is right. And then, out of grace, God gives us the faith to accept that offer because, self-absorbed sinners that we are, we don't have the faith to do it. It's still our free-will choice, but we couldn't make that choice without God's help. The only difference between Methodists and CPs here is that Methodists usually say we are "saved by faith," whereas CPs say we are "saved by grace" (Confession of Faith 4.03, 4.04, 4.08, 4.15). Since faith is a gift of God's grace, though, either phrase is accurate.

Methodists believe that Christians can lose their salvation; not just through sinning, but through unconfessed (and therefore unforgiven) sin; or by simply choosing to give up one's faith. CPs disagree. We put the emphasis on God's action in salvation, and what God does sticks. We can't undo our salvation any more than we could un-create a tree. We call this the preservation of believers (Confession 4.24-4.25). Some Methodists, however, do say that this point of their doctrine can be interpreted either way.

13

Some Methodists, mostly those also in the Holiness/Pentecostal movement, believe as did John Wesley that Christians can achieve "Christian Perfection," a sinless life. This isn't done through one's own strength of faith or spiritual resolve, though, but only by the power of the Holy Spirit. CPs say we "never achieve sinless perfection in this life," but the Holy Spirit does continually makes us more Christ-like, as we strive to become so (Confession 4.22).

APPLYING THE LESSON TO YOUR OWN LIFE
Multiple small-membership United Methodist congregations in the same area will share a pastor, either having him/her preach at each church every Sunday or with the congregations alternating which Sundays they hold services. What do you see as possible benefits of this arrangement? Possible detriments? Possible dangers? Could any CP congregations in your presbytery employ a similar arrangement?

Are you familiar with the logo of the CP Church, adopted in 2006, and its meaning? (See it at cumberland.org, under "Our Logo.") The UMC logo is known around the world. Is ours? How visible does your congregation make our denominational logo? Why is it important for a denomination to have an easily-recognized logo?

Which do you think is more important in reaching out to the community: a congregation's name or its denominational affiliation? For example, which do you think is a more effective name for a congregation: Grace Church (a Cumberland Presbyterian congregation) or Grace Cumberland Presbyterian Church? Why?

THE CHURCH DOWN THE STREET:
THE CHURCH WITH THE RED FLAMES ON THEIR SIGN

SCRIPTURE
JOHN 3:16, ACTS 2:1-3, 1 TIMOTHY 3:1-3

LEADER PREP

RESOURCE LIST
- Bibles
- Paper for each student
- Pencils for each student
- Slips of paper with John Wesley facts
- "What's in a Cross" worksheet for each student
- Music and words for "Hymns of Charles Wesley"
- Art supplies to be used in the "What's in a Cross" creative activity: pens, markers, clay, fabric and paint, magazine pages, scissors, glue, etc.
- Copy of the "Social Creed Litany" for each student (or projector and slides)

BEFORE LESSON

Get 10 slips of paper and write one of the John Wesley facts from the "Get to Know John Wesley" list on Page 20 or make a copy and cut them out. Do not number the slips of paper, since students will be trying to guess the order in which the events happened.

Make a copy of the "What's in a Cross" worksheet on Page 22 for each student.

Make a copy of the "Social Creed Litany" on Page 21 for each student, or get a projector and make slides with the words to the litany, so students can follow along.

If you are using the "Hymns of Charles Wesley" activity, choose what song(s) you want to use. Find the music and a way to play it, as well as words if you want students to sing along.

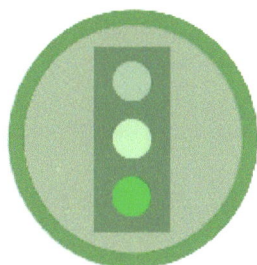

GET STARTED

GET STARTED (10 minutes)

SAY:Today we are learning about the Methodist denominations. Does anyone have any experience with, or know much about, the United Methodist Church? Allow a little bit of time for students to share their stories.

SAY:To start our lesson today, we are going to learn a little bit about the founder of the Methodist movement, John Wesley.

Pass out the pieces of paper with facts about John Wesley (the underlined portions on the "Get to Know John Wesley list on Page 20) to the students, or have them all on one large piece of paper at the front of the room.

If you have more than 10 students, some may have to share facts. If you have less, some students may get more than one fact. Have the students work together to try and guess what order these events happened in John Wesley's life. Once they finish, use the "Answer Key" on Page 19 to tell them which ones they got correct and let them try again. When they get it correct (or give up), spend a couple of minutes sharing some of the extra facts from the "Answer Key" about each event in John Wesley's life.

LISTEN UP (20 minutes)
When you are ready, start this portion of the lesson by saying, "The Methodist movement has changed a lot since John Wesley was alive. The denomination has grown, split, and reunited multiple times, and there are now many different denominations that share the name, beliefs, and history of the Methodist Church. The largest and most common branch of Methodism today is the United Methodist Church. The United Methodist Church is similar to our own denomination, but it is also different in many ways, including structure, government, and theological beliefs. Today we are going to use three different scriptures as a basis to learn a little bit more about the United Methodist Church, and how it compares to our own Cumberland Presbyterian Church."

LISTEN UP

Have someone read John 3:16, "For God so loved the world that he gave his only Son, so that everyone who believes in him may not perish but may have eternal life."

SAY: The main theological differences between the Methodists and Cumberland Presbyterians have to do with salvation. UMs believe that Christ died on the cross to offer us salvation, but humans are the ones who choose whether or not to accept that gift, and salvation comes from that acceptance. CPs also believe that Christ died on the cross to offer us salvation and humans have free will to accept or reject that gift, but God is the one who helps us to accept the gift and receive salvation."

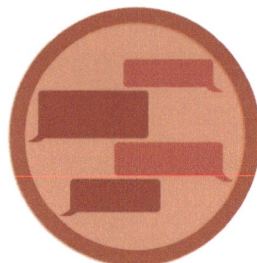

DISCUSSION QUESTIONS

ASK: What do you see as the difference between these two approaches to salvation? Why is this difference important?

If students have trouble understanding these different ways of looking at salvation, use this or another similar example: Imagine heaven being like a cloud floating above the earth. Sin has created a large gap separating us from going into the cloud and being in relationship with God. When Jesus died on the cross for our sins, he built a ladder to bridge that gap, so that we can once again be with God. The UMs would say that the ladder is always just sitting there, and anyone who chooses to can climb the ladder and receive salvation by being with God. The CPs would say that Jesus is at the foot of the ladder calling out to people, and that when someone accepts his call, he leads them up the ladder and into salvation.

ASK: What do you see as the role of God in each of these beliefs? What about the role of humans?

Another salvation difference between UMs and CPs is that we believe in the assurance of salvation: once God has saved a person, it is permanent and nothing can happen to change that. UMs believe that it is possible for a Christian to lose their salvation, either as a result of sinning or because they choose to turn and walk away from God.

ASK: What do you see as the role of God in each of these beliefs? What about the role of humans?

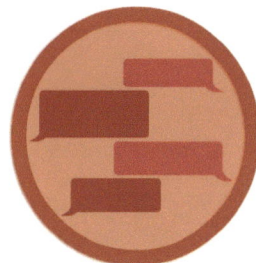

DISCUSSION QUESTIONS

Read or have someone read 1 Timothy 3:1-3, "The saying is sure: whoever aspires to the office of bishop desires a noble task. Now a bishop must be above reproach, married only once, temperate, sensible, respectable, hospitable, an apt teacher, not a drunkard, not violent but gentle, not quarrelsome, and not a lover of money."

There are also differences in governing bodies within the UMC and CPC. The UMs have bishops and other paid individuals who are in leadership positions, while the CPs rely on governing bodies like presbyteries to lead. Pastors within the UMs are also employees of the denomination, and those paid leaders are responsible for appointing them and moving them to churches where they think the pastor would be a good fit. Individual churches within the CPC are responsible for finding and hiring their own pastors.

ASK: What are some of the advantages and disadvantages to each of these governing systems?

ASK: How does the scripture from 1 Timothy about the responsibilities of leaders in the Early Church relate to church leaders today?

ASK: What are some other difference and similarities you might know of between CPs and the United Methodists?

DISCUSSION QUESTIONS

ASK: What questions do you have about the United Methodist Church that we have not discussed?

NOW WHAT? (15 minutes)
Choose one of the following options.

NOW WHAT

OPTION1: "What's in a Cross" Worksheet
Give each student a copy of the worksheet. In groups of two to four, have students look at the logos and their explanations for each denomination. Ask them to consider what information they would want to communicate about their own faith with a logo. On the back of the worksheet, on another piece of paper, or with whatever art supplies you want to provide (clay, fabric and paint, magazine pages, etc.), have each group create their own logo that demonstrates what they think is most important to convey to others about their faith. If time allows, have the groups share their projects with one another.

OPTION 2: Notes to a Friend
Give each student (or pair of students) paper and a pen. Tell them to think of a friend who is United Methodist or to make one up if they do not have a UM friend. Have them write a note to their friend explaining why they are Cumberland Presbyterian. Encourage them to use the information they learned today about the UMC to help explain to their friend what they believe, and why they choose the CP denomination. Make sure to keep the letters positive—they are learning to articulate their own faith, not bashing someone else's beliefs. Allow some students to share their letters if you have time.

LIVE IT

LIVE IT (10 minutes)
Choose one of the following ways to close out the lesson:

1) Wesley's General Rules:
John Wesley had three general rules that he lived by and encouraged his followers to make a regular practice in their own lives. These Three General Rules are paraphrased to say:

1. DO NO HARM
2. DO GOOD
3. STAY IN LOVE WITH GOD

ASK: What do each of these rules mean to you?

ASK: What is one way you can try to live out each of these rules this week?

Ask for three volunteers to pray as you dismiss. Give each of them a rule, and have them pray that your students can apply that rule to their lives in this next week.

2) SOCIAL CREED LITANY
The UMC has created a social creed to help guide the way they interact with the world, with God's creation, and with one another. This creed is summarized in the following litany, which we will use to close out our time together. Let this prayer be our prayer today, and allow these words to change the way you interact with the world around you this coming week.

Hymns of Charles Wesley: This could be used along with, or in place of, a Get Started or Live it activity. Though not as well-known as his brother John, Charles Wesley was a founder of the Methodist Church. One of his valuable contributions to the early Methodist movement was songwriting. In his lifetime, Charles wrote over 9,000 songs and poems, many of which are still popular among Christians today. Choose a Charles Wesley song to listen to or sing together in an act of worship. Some popular ones to choose from: "A Charge to Keep I Have," "Christ the Lord is Risen Today," "Come Thou Long Expected Jesus," "Hark! the Herald Angels Sing," "Love Divine All Loves Excelling," "O For a Thousand Tongues to Sing"

NOTES

Resources used in compiling background information: ame-church.com, christianity.com, faithcommunitiestoday.org, Handbook of Denominations in the United States by Frank Mead, thecmechurch.org, umc.org, Westminster Dictionary of Theological Terms, www.wesleyschapel.org.uk, www.christianitytoday.com/ch/1983/issue2/218.html, www.cumberland.org. Pictures used: John Wesley by Paul Wilkinson - https://goo.gl/wbeK9r, To the Pleiades by Mike Lewinski - https://goo.gl/Wiih1B, John Wesley by Paul Wilkinson - https://goo.gl/Sa0qO0, Bildnis des Ioannes Wesleyus - Universitätsbibliothek Leipzig https://goo.gl/Y460Zv, https://goo.gl/WV3rVG, Prairie dandelions by Loren Kerns https://goo.gl/KExeZw

GET TO KNOW JOHN WESLEY

1. He was born on June 28th, 1703–He was born the fifteenth of nineteen children to Rev. Samuel and Susanna Wesley.

2. Almost killed when the church manse/rectory/parsonage/house catches on fire with him trapped inside. 1709–He is 5 years old at the time and felt that he was saved for a purpose, that God had protected him for a reason.

3. Taught classes on logic, the classics, and divinity at Lincoln College in Oxford. 1726–He became a fellow and taught after graduating with a B.A. and while working on his M.A.

4. Became an ordained Priest in the Anglican Church. 1728

5. Travels to America. 1735–John and his brother Charles travel to Georgia where John serves as a chaplain to settlers and missionary to Native Americans. On the journey they encounter a powerful storm at sea, and John says that he and the other English men were overcome with fear, but he was impressed and humbled to see that the German Moravian missionaries sang hymns to God and remained calm.

6. Experiences a powerful assurance of salvation at Aldersgate Street. 1738–He wrote in his journal, "In the evening I went very unwillingly to a society in Aldersgate Street, where one was reading Luther's Preface to the Epistle to the Romans. About a quarter before nine, while he was describing the change which God works in the heart through faith in Christ, I felt my heart strangely warmed. I felt I did trust in Christ, Christ alone for salvation; and an assurance was given me that He had taken away my sins, even mine, and saved me from the law of sin and death."

7. Preaches his first open-air sermon. 1739–He said that before this moment he thought it "almost a sin" to save souls outside of a church, but after this he realized that he could reach more people by preaching in the fields and meeting people where they were.

8. First Methodist conference is held. 1744–This was held at the Foundry Chapel in London, and the country was divided into Methodist districts.

9. Visits Ireland for the first time. 1747–This was his first of 42 trips preaching in Ireland.

10. At age 87, he dies in his London home on March 2nd. 1791–It is said that in his lifetime, he likely rode 250,000 miles on horseback, gave away 30,000 pounds, and preached more than 40,000 sermons.

GET TO KNOW JOHN WESLEY

Travels to America.

First Methodist conference is held.

Taught classes on logic, the classics, and divinity at Lincoln College in Oxford.

He was born on June 28th.

Experiences a powerful assurance of salvation at Aldersgate Street.

At age 87, he dies in his London home on March 2nd.

Visits Ireland for the first time.

Became an ordained Priest in the Anglican Church.

Preaches his first open-air sermon.

Almost killed when the church manse/ rectory/parsonage/house catches on fire with him trapped inside.

SOCIAL CREED LITANY

GOD IN THE SPIRIT REVEALED IN JESUS CHRIST,
CALLS US BY GRACE
  TO BE RENEWED IN THE IMAGE OF OUR CREATOR,
  THAT WE MAY BE ONE
  IN DIVINE LOVE FOR THE WORLD.
TODAY IS THE DAY
GOD CARES FOR THE INTEGRITY OF CREATION,
  WILLS THE HEALING AND WHOLENESS OF ALL LIFE,
  WEEPS AT THE PLUNDER OF EARTH'S GOODNESS.
AND SO SHALL WE.
TODAY IS THE DAY
GOD EMBRACES ALL HUES OF HUMANITY,
  DELIGHTS IN DIVERSITY AND DIFFERENCE,
  FAVORS SOLIDARITY TRANSFORMING STRANGERS INTO FRIENDS.
AND SO SHALL WE.
 TODAY IS THE DAY
GOD CRIES WITH THE MASSES OF STARVING PEOPLE,
  DESPISES GROWING DISPARITY BETWEEN RICH AND POOR,
  DEMANDS JUSTICE FOR WORKERS IN THE MARKETPLACE.
AND SO SHALL WE.
TODAY IS THE DAY
GOD DEPLORES VIOLENCE IN OUR HOMES AND STREETS,
  REBUKES THE WORLD'S WARRING MADNESS,
  HUMBLES THE POWERFUL AND LIFTS UP THE LOWLY.
AND SO SHALL WE.
TODAY IS THE DAY
GOD CALLS FOR NATIONS AND PEOPLES TO LIVE IN PEACE,
  CELEBRATES WHERE JUSTICE AND MERCY EMBRACE,
  EXULTS WHEN THE WOLF GRAZES WITH THE LAMB.
AND SO SHALL WE.
TODAY IS THE DAY
GOD BRINGS GOOD NEWS TO THE POOR,
  PROCLAIMS RELEASE TO THE CAPTIVES,
  GIVES SIGHT TO THE BLIND, AND
  SETS THE OPPRESSED FREE.
AND SO SHALL WE.

From The Book of Discipline of The United Methodist Church - 2012.
Copyright 2012 by The United Methodist Publishing House.

WHAT'S IN A CROSS?

CUMBERLAND PRESBYTERIAN CROSS

The CP cross represents Christians coming together to become the Body of Christ.

The cross is made up of four people joining together in community and facing outward into the world.

The hands are connected to make a circle, that represents both the world and the never-ending gift of God's grace and love.

The negative space within the circle resembles four communion cups, to represent the Cup of Salvation that we drink during communion being sent out to the four corners of the world.

UNITED METHODIST CROSS

The UM cross represents our connection to God.

The traditional cross represents Jesus' love for us and our chance at salvation through the cross.

The flame represents the gift of the Holy Spirit on Pentecost as told in Acts 2:1-3—"When the day of Pentecost had come, they were all together in one place. And suddenly from heaven there came a sound like the rush of a violent wind, and it filled the entire house where they were sitting. Divided tongues, as of fire, appeared among them, and a tongue rested on each of them."

The flame also resembles John Wesley's transforming moment when he sensed God's presence and felt his heart "strangely warmed."

The two tongues of the flame also represent the two denominations (The Methodist Church and the Evangelical United Brethren Church) to form the United Methodists.

FAITH OUT LOUD

THE CHURCH DOWN THE STREET:
THE CHURCH KNOWN AS THE "FROZEN CHOSEN"

BY NATHAN WHEELER AND ANDY McCLUNG

SCRIPTURE
ACTS 14:23 & 1 CORINTHIANS 12:4-13

THEME
An overview of the Presbyterian family of churches, with a brief comparison to the Cumberland Presbyterian Church.

CONNECTING TO YOUR STUDENTS

Some of your students may have met someone—maybe an unchurched person or someone from out of town—who confused your Cumberland Presbyterian church and the Presbyterian church down the street. This happens a lot. Some folks even see "First Cumberland Presbyterian Church" and think it's a Presbyterian Church named "First Cumberland."

If your students have visited the other Presbyterian church(es) in town, they may be confused themselves, wondering what difference there is between the two (or more) denominations. They may even wonder why, if all these churches are Presbyterian, they can't just all come together to form one congregation.

Some of your students may have no idea what it even means to be part of the Presbyterian family of churches. Since these different denominations share roots and some theology, but are indeed different organizations, you might find the analogy of cousins useful.

EXPLAINING THE TOPIC

There are about twenty different types of Presbyterian denominations in the U.S., and even more in other countries. After the Reformation in the early 1500s, Protestants began to group together according to their beliefs. Some, drawn to the theology of John Calvin, came together in the mid-1500s and were further influenced by John Knox (the Father of Presbyterianism) to establish the first Presbyterian Church. Since then, many denominational "branches" have grown from this "vine." Some of these denominations are big; some are small. While they all share roots, they can be quite different from one another. Here we'll consider only the ones most likely to be down the street from your church. First, let's note what they all have in common.

The Greek word for "elder" led to the English words "presbyter," "presbytery," and "presbyterian." Presbyterian churches have elders who represent the people in church government (thus distinguishing it from the congregational form of government). There is no bishop (thus distinguishing it from the episcopal form of government). The churches are organized into presbyteries. Authority is invested in the community, shared by clergy and elders.

Theologically, Presbyterians share a deep respect for, and emphasis on, the sovereignty of God. They use confessions of faith to declare their beliefs, and written rules to define their polity (governmental structure and practices). They all recognize baptism and communion as sacraments, practice infant baptism, and baptize by pouring/sprinkling (primarily). They all require education for ministers.

Of the 56 people to sign the U.S. Declaration of Independence, at least 11 were Presbyterian.

The Associate Reformed Presbyterian Church has about 40,000 members in about 300 congregations in the U.S. and Canada. They operate on a $7 million annual budget. They use the Westminster Confession of Faith and are boldly conservative (i.e. right-wing) in their theological and social stances. They ordain only men as elders and ministers.

The Cumberland Presbyterian Church in America, which is predominantly African-American, has 114 congregations in 8 states. The denomination began in 1874, when former slaves who had joined their owners' CP congregations while still slaves created their own denomination. (There's an entire Faith Out Loud lesson on the relationship between these two denominations: "Siblings in Faith.") We share the same Confession of Faith and Constitution and participate in many joint ministries together. Many persons in both denominations hope to reunite as one denomination.

The Evangelical Presbyterian Church began in 1981, when a group of ministers and elders in two other Presbyterian denominations became tired of how liberal their denominations had become. Seeing no hope to change that, they started a new denomination that took the Bible seriously, acknowledged the theology of the historic confessions, and was evangelical. They started with 12 congregations and now have about 550— the growth coming from church planting and established congregations transferring from other Presbyterian denominations. The EPC allows each presbytery, of which there are 13, to decide whether or not they ordain women as elders and ministers; at least one congregation has changed presbyteries in order to call a female pastor.

The Presbyterian Church in America also separated from its parent denomination over distaste for liberalism; however, it did so in 1973. Part of the reason for this separation was the impending reunion of the two branches of the Presbyterian Church that separated over the socio-political differences that contributed to the American Civil War. Those who became the PCA didn't want to reunite with the liberal Presbyterians. Thus, this denomination is firmly on the far right of the socio-political-theological spectrum. They have over 340,000 members in about 2,000 congregations, mostly in the U.S., with some in Canada, Japan, Korea, and Europe. They ordain only men as elders and ministers, and hold firmly to the Westminster Confession of Faith. In 1982, the Reformed Presbyterian Church Evangelical Synod joined them.

The Presbyterian Church (USA) has 1.6 million members in about 10,000 congregations arranged in 171 presbyteries. To put this size in perspective: the PC(USA) loses about as many members each year as the CP church has in total.) About $2.5 billion flows through the church each year. The PC(USA) began in 1983, when two separate Presbyterian denominations reunited as one, the previous split having happened at the beginning of the American Civil War. Nonetheless, this denomination can trace its lineage to the beginnings of Presbyterianism in North America. The PC(USA) is generally seen as liberal, but it's probably more accurate to say that of the leadership than the people; church members typically fall all along the conservative-liberal spectrum. This church ordains both women and men as elders and ministers and recently removed the rule that restricted marriage to a man and a woman. Of the denominations listed here, this one is probably the most culturally diverse.

Presbyterianism is popular in Korea, and there is a Korean American Presbyterian Church in the U.S., as well as predominantly Korean-American congregations within other Presbyterian denominations... including ours.

That's a lot of denominations, a lot of splits and reunions. Why we can't all just get along and be one denomination? Well, to quote Ed Reeves, a CP elder at First CP Church, Chattanooga: "For the same reason Baskin-Robbins has 31 flavors." In other words, people are going to disagree about some things, so it's best to find the denomination and congregation in which you can most joyfully worship God, most effectively grow in faith, and best use your gifts and abilities in ministry.

THEOLOGICAL UNDERPINNINGS
One thing that theologically distinguishes the CP Church from most other Presbyterians is that we don't believe in predestination. That's the belief that God decided long ago exactly who would be saved and who wouldn't. This belief is clearly set forth in the Westminster Confession of Faith; disagreement with it is part of what led to the founding of the Cumberland Presbyterian Church in 1810 (See the Faith Out Loud Lesson "Oops, We Made a Church!")

Today, most members of the ARP, EPC, or PCA Church probably know their church officially teaches predestination, and likely would agree. Members of the PC(USA), however, hold a variety of beliefs about predestination, because the PC(USA) uses a whole book of confessions, including the Westminster Confession of Faith. Ministers, elders, and session may choose from these confessions whatever they like best. Critics of this practice might say that having too many confessions is the same as having none. Because of its origins, the EPC says each congregation owns its building. The PC(USA) and the CPC say the congregation uses and takes care of its building, but ultimately the presbytery owns it (Constitution 3.30-3.35). The latter is the traditional arrangement in Presbyterianism and reflects the theology of Acts 4:32-35.

Many Presbyterian denominations hold strictly to the Westminster Confession of Faith. The Cumberland Presbyterian Church developed our own Confession of Faith. All CP elders and ministers have stated, in their ordination vows, that they "sincerely receive and adopt the Confession of Faith...as containing the essential doctrines taught in the holy scriptures" (Constitution 2.92, 3.36).

Presbyterian church government is theological as well; the representative form of government is based on the synagogue system of ancient Judaism. The word "elder" appears in the Bible.

APPLYING THE LESSON TO YOUR OWN LIFE
Have you ever had to explain the difference between your church and another Presbyterian church? If so, what did you say? If not, what would you say if you found yourself in that position?

What do you think of Mr. Reeves' Baskin-Robbins analogy?

Which do you think is more common: someone attends/joins a congregation because the theology suits them, or someone attends/joins a congregation where they feel welcomed and then they adopt the congregation's theology? What problems, both practical and spiritual, might arise if someone attends/joins a congregation but does not adopt the theology?

How might it change the CP Church to be as big as the PC(USA)?

How well do you think the typical member of your congregation knows our Confession of Faith? If knowledge is lacking, consider asking your session to schedule a series of studies. Hubert Morrow's "A Covenant of Grace" is an excellent resource to use.

JUST IN CASE
It's unlikely, but one of your students might ask about the denomination called the Upper Cumberland Presbyterian Church. In 1952, the Revised Standard Version of the Bible was published, a modernized translation of the Standard (or King James) Version. The National Council of Churches (NCC) was involved. The 1953 CP General Assembly refused to drop membership in the NCC, as some CPs requested, namely because we weren't a member of the NCC. The CPs opposed to the NCC and the RSV ended up forming their own, ultra-conservative denomination: the Upper Cumberland Presbyterian (the "Upper" coming from their location near the "upper" portion of the Cumberland River, east of Nashville). They adapted the CP Confession of Faith and named the King James Version as their official Bible. While information is hard to find, it seems this denomination is quite small—just a few churches near Gallatin, Tennessee.

DIGGING DEEPER
The Westminster Confession of Faith was intended for the Anglican Church, not Presbyterians. It was written over a few years and finished in 1646 by a committee of British men, some from the House of Lords (inherited positions), some from the House of Commons (elected positions), and some from the clergy (including some Presbyterians). They met at Westminster Abbey in London. By the time they finished, the British crown had changed hands, and the new monarch shifted the nation back to Catholicism. Scottish folks liked the Confession and used it in the Presbyterian Church there. Although Presbyterians had been here for almost a century, the first presbytery in the U.S. (or what would become the U.S.) was established in 1706. In 1729, that Church adopted the Westminster Confession of Faith as its official doctrine.

THE CHURCH DOWN THE STREET:
THE CHURCH KNOWN AS THE "FROZEN CHOSEN"

SCRIPTURE
ACTS 14:23 & 1 CORINTHIANS 12:4-13

LEADER PREP

RESOURCE LIST
- "Famous Presbyterian" • Hymns to play

- "Presbyterian Lingo" • Party decorations

- a way to play "Wanna Party Like a Presbyterian" https://goo.gl/Fdxktd or download the song by visiting http://www.partylikeapresbyterian.com

- Newsprint with markers, or dry erase board with marker

- Paper and pens/pencils • Optional: invite session member to come and answer questions

BEFORE THE LESSON
Set up a speaker or plug your computer into a monitor, and cue up the song "Wanna Party Like A Presbyterian." If you are feeling adventurous, play it as students arrive. Set up the room like a Presbyterian party. Decorate using a choir robe, a hymnal or two, offering plate, Celtic crosses, pictures of John Calvin, John Knox, Patrick Hamilton, Huldrych Zwingli, Liturgical colors (purple, green, red, white) and stained glass windows or pictures just to name a few items.

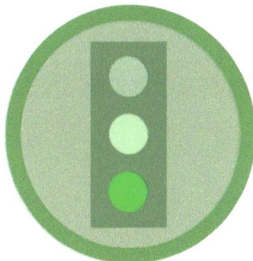

GET STARTED (20 minutes)
As students arrive, play the song "Wanna Party Like A Presbyterian" (download the song or play the short video from YouTube. Find links in the resource section). After they have a chance to sit down and take in the room,

ASK: What does it mean to party like a Presbyterian?

ASK: When you think of the word Presbyterian, what words come to mind?

DISCUSSION QUESTIONS

SAY: The song playing is meant to be funny, a joke because most folks don't think "party" when they think of Presbyterians. In fact, some say Presbyterians are the "frozen chosen."

ASK: What do you think the phrase "frozen chosen" means?

SAY: That phrase comes from the general sense that Presbyterians are boring. Our way of doing things—sermons, hymns, liturgy, Bible study—they are just plain boring. In fact, one of the things that you might agree with is that learning to be Presbyterian is boring. Confirmation class anyone? Today's lesson is on Presbyterians.

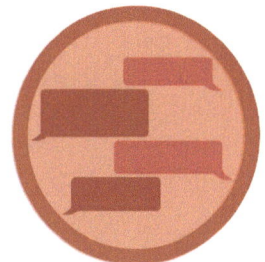

PARTY GAMES

Feel free to choose to play one or all the party games provided. I would highly suggest using the song "Wanna Party Like A Presbyterian" during all the party games.

PARTY GAME #1 - Name that Presbyterian.
This game is simple; you will name facts about a famous Presbyterian, and the first person to call out the right name wins. You can find names and facts on the handout called "Famous Presbyterians."

PARTY GAME #2 - Hymn Musical Chairs
Have students form a circle of chairs with one less chair than students. Choose a couple of popular hymns to play as students walk around chairs. When you stop the hymns, students must find a chair and sit down. The student left standing is out of the game. Remove one chair each round until there is one winner.

PARTY GAME #3 - Presbyterian Lingo
Describe something that is used in Presbyterian circles, and have students guess what you are describing. You can find descriptions and terms on the handout "Presbyterian Lingo."

LISTEN UP (20 minutes)

After finishing up playing party games, gather your group back together. Have them open their Bibles to Acts 14:23. Have one of the students read the text.

SAY: One of the ways Presbyterians are different from other denominations is how they are in community with one another. In the scripture, we read about Paul and Barnabas appointing elders in churches.

ASK: What does elder mean?

LISTEN UP

SAY: The term elder comes from a Greek term presbyter (sounds familiar) meaning old/older. In the church, elders are elected by a congregation to share in the government and leadership of the church.

In a Presbyterian church, the congregation elects elders, and together they make up the session of the church. The session of a church helps to make the final decisions on matters pertaining to the church and are called the spiritual leaders of the church.

It might be good to invite a session member to this meeting to speak about being an elder and to answer any questions.

A group of churches are called presbyteries. These presbyteries meet several times a year to conduct business. The members of presbyteries are ministers and elders from local congregations. They meet to examine new candidates for ministry, approve folks for ordination, and hear reports from various boards and committees.

A group of presbyteries is called a synod. Finally, elected ministers and elders from presbyteries make up the General Assembly. These assemblies happen annually, or every other year, depending on the Presbyterian denomination. General Assembly, synods, presbyteries, and sessions are vital to sustaining the community called Presbyterian.

This looks different from many churches down the street. Other denominations structure their community around a congregational or episcopal form of government.

You can read more about this in the lessons about Baptists (Pages 3-10) and Methodists (Pages 11-22)

ASK: So, what is different about Presbyterians? Why aren't we all one denomination?

SAY: One of the ways we are different is who can be an elder or who can be a minister. Some Presbyterian denominations only allow men to be elders or ordained ministers. Others allow men and women to serve as elders and ordained ministers.

This is called a complementarian view versus an egalitarian view.

A complementarian view holds that men and women have different roles. These roles are biblically based and state that women may not hold authority over a man, which some interpret to mean women cannot be elders or ordained ministers.

An egalitarian view says that men and women were created equally. This view is biblically based and would argue that men and women may serve as both elders and ordained ministers in the church.

In the Confession of Faith of the Cumberland Presbyterian Church, it states, "the office of elder may be male or female, young or old" (2.73). It is also the practice of the CPC to ordain men and women as ministers of word and sacrament.

ASK: What do you think about these views? What do you think should be the requirements of an elder or minister of a church? Should gender matter?

Have your group write what they think should be the requirements on a board or piece of paper. After the lesson, share that with the elders and ministers of your church.

DISCUSSION QUESTIONS

SAY: Another difference between Presbyterians is a view called predestination.

ASK: What is predestination?

Predestination is a multilayered word. As far as Presbyterians go, it can mean a variety of things. The part of this theological concept that causes divisions is an interpretation of the word that says God has predetermined who will go to heaven and who will go to hell. This is a stark contrast to the idea of free will—that all people have a choice to accept salvation or not.

This concept was articulated by John Calvin, one of the founders of Presbyterianism. It is also one of the main reasons there are so many different Presbyterian churches today.

ASK: Do you think we have free will, or do you believe God has predestined some to follow and others not to follow God?

Cumberland Presbyterians are a hybrid of Calvinism and Arminianism. We have a "whosoever will" theology that some call "medium theology."

There is more information in the Leader Insight section on Pages 24-26. If you have time you might want to share some of that information with your group.

NOW WHAT? (15 minutes)
More Alike Than Unalike

Have each person grab a partner. Have them make a list with their partner of all the things that are alike about them. This can be physical traits, personality traits or commonalities of their lives (i.e. go to the same school, like the same music). After they have done this, have them make a second list of the things that are unalike. (Don't forget to play "Wanna Party Like A Presbyterian")

NOW WHAT

Once finished, have the groups share what is alike and unalike. As they share, write on newsprint or dry erase board the things that are alike and unalike. After all groups have shared, take some time and circle or underline the things that were the same for everyone.

SAY: We all spend lots of our time looking for what is different in one another. What if we spent the same amount of time, or even more time, looking for what is the same in one another? What difference would that make?

Despite our differences, we are more alike than unalike. Though our denominations meet in different buildings with different ways of doing things, we are the universal church. We are unified by the God who loves us, the Son that saved us, and the Spirit who guides us.

ASK: What could you do to help others see past their differences and embrace their sameness?

LIVE IT (5 minutes)

SAY: As we close our time together, let's end by reading 1 Corinthians 12:4-13 (NRSV).

[4] Now there are varieties of gifts, but the same Spirit; [5] and there are varieties of services, but the same Lord; [6] and there are varieties of activities, but it is the same God who activates all of them in everyone. [7] To each is given the manifestation of the Spirit for the common good. [8] To one is given through the Spirit the utterance of wisdom, and to another the utterance of knowledge according to the same Spirit, [9] to another faith by the same Spirit, to another gifts of healing by the one Spirit, [10] to another the working of miracles, to another prophecy, to another the discernment of spirits, to another various kinds of tongues, to another the interpretation of tongues. [11] All these are activated by one and the same Spirit, who allots to each one individually just as the Spirit chooses. [12] For just as the body is one and has many members, and all the members of the body, though many, are one body, so it is with Christ. [13] For in the one Spirit we were all baptized into one body—Jews or Greeks, slaves or free—and we were all made to drink of one Spirit.

CLOSING PRAYER:

God, remind us that there are varieties of Christians, but we are of the same Spirit. Help us learn to live in harmony with one another and with you. Amen.

NOTES

Resources used in compiling background information: A People Called Cumberland Presbyterians by Ben Barrus, et al; arpchurch.org; epc.org; Handbook of Denominations in the United States by Frank Mead; pcusa.org; thearda.com; usconstitution.net, www.youtube.com/watch?v=Xh8DB6Qi7qo, http://www.partylikeapresbyterian.com, Confession of Faith, The Presbyterian Handbook Geneva Press, Holy Bible (NRSV). Pictures used: John Knox Statue by Unknown - http://goo.gl/2xqumc, Disobedient whale by Loozrboy https://goo.gl/dn1EHF

FAMOUS PRESBYTERIANS

Donald Trump: A wealthy business man, who gained notoriety for his reality TV show where he says to contestants, "You're fired".

Ronald Reagan: An actor, who became governor of California and later President of the United States.

David Letterman: An American comedian who had a long career on TV as a late night talk show host.

Mark Twain: A novelist and writer who wrote Tom Sawyer and Huckleberry Finn.

Fred Rogers: A TV actor who had a long running children's program where he invited you to be his neighbor.

Shirley Temple: A child star who made lots of movies back in the day that featured her dancing and singing.

Condoleezza Rice: Former Secretary of State under George W. Bush. An avid football fan, she is one of the members of the college football playoff selection committee.

Sheryl Crow: A musician known for songs like "Soak up the Sun" and "If It Makes You Happy."

JK Rowling: Famous author of the Harry Potter book series.

PRESBYTERIAN LINGO

General Assembly: The church's highest governing body, including elders and clergy commissioners from all the denomination's presbyteries

Synod: The church's governing body, made up of presbyteries from a specific region

Presbytery: The church's governing body, composed of clergy and elected elders from a specific region

Elder: An elected representative in a local church

Session: The group of elders from a local church

Stated Clerk: The person who functions as the official record keeper

Book of Confession: A book that expresses what Presbyterians believe

The Apostles' Creed: The most widely used confession of faith in Presbyterian churches

Liturgy: The stuff we recite or repeat in worship

FAITH OUT LOUD

THE CHURCH DOWN THE STREET:
IS THAT CHURCH DOWN THE STREET CHRISTIAN?

BY NATHAN WHEELER and ANDY McCLUNG

SCRIPTURE
MATTHEW 7:21-23, JOHN 14:6, 2 PETER 2:1-3

THEME
An overview of worshiping communities whose Christianity is often questioned, and their compatibility with Cumberland Presbyterianism.

CONNECTING TO YOUR STUDENTS

Some churched teens have been taught not to trust or accept any religions outside of mainstream Christianity; some have been taught that all religions are the same—different and equally valid paths to God; and some have been taught nothing at all about other religions. Your students may all share the same mindset on such things, or they may have a wide range of opinions.

Those students who are suspicious of, or outright reject, overtly non-Christian religions may still be confused about worshiping communities which appear more like a Christian church than, say, an Islamic mosque. Your students may have classmates who belong to such religious groups.

Church-raised teens may be tempted to participate in one or more of these groups as a way of searching for their own identity, rebelling against parents, or for a novel religious experience.

For all these reasons, this lesson seeks to tread lightly while still affirming the truth of Christianity.

EXPLAINING THE TOPIC

Non-Christian religions—Judaism and Islam, for example—are not the focus of this lesson, but rather those worshiping communities that may be down the street from your church...and it's not quite clear if they're Christian. This uncertainty may come from our ignorance or different understandings of what it means to be Christian. It's important to note that simply practicing one's faith differently from us does not, in and of itself, make a group non-Christian.

Christian Scientists are members of the Church of Christ, Science, best known for relying on prayer rather than medicine. True healing, they say, comes from God. Refusing medicine is not required of members; they're officially free to make their own decisions about healthcare. Everything seems centered on healing for them, probably because the founder started this movement after being healed from injuries sustained in a fall. Her followers seem to hold her writings as equally important as the Bible. This group acknowledges one God, Christ, the Holy Spirit, that humankind is made in God's image, and that humankind is saved through Christ. But they say Jesus' crucifixion and resurrection "uplift faith to understand eternal Life," not that these events atoned for our sins. All their talk of Jesus is about him as an example to follow, not as a savior to accept.

This group believes disease and material things are unreal delusions; only spiritual things really exist and matter. Christianity teaches that God created the material world, and that each human is equally mind, body, and spirit; without any one of which we're not human, which is why we believe in the resurrection of the body after death. Christianity also teaches self-sacrifice for the common good, but this group seems overly focused on what God can do for the individual.

Jehovah's Witnesses say they're Christian, because they follow the teachings of Jesus Christ, whom they believe is the key to salvation, and in whose name persons are baptized and prayers are offered. But they don't think Jesus was God incarnate. He was a human who lived in perfect obedience to God, and who now rules God's heavenly kingdom. They deny the Trinity, and believe they're the only true religion.

Critics deride this group's claim (drawn from Revelation 7:4-8) that only 144,000 people will be saved. The actual teaching, however, is that 144,000 will be "co-rulers" with Jesus in Heaven; all other humans who "prove themselves obedient to God" will live on a perfected Earth after the resurrection. Those not worthy simply cease to exist, as there is no place of eternal punishment.

Jehovah's Witnesses support everything they believe with scripture. They emphasize moral living and have a strong emphasis on sharing their faith with others.

Seventh Day Adventists believe the Bible teaches 28 "Fundamental Doctrines"; the Bible was inspired by God; God is triune; Jesus was God incarnate, fully human and fully divine, and died for our sins; and it is through him alone that we are saved. They focus a lot on the end times and have specific beliefs about what happens after death.

Adventists believe the end of the world and Christ's second coming are near, and it's their duty to warn everyone, but they've never set a specific date. Saturday, the Sabbath, is their holy day, because the Bible says so. They practice foot washing because, Jesus said to (John 13:14).

Mormons prefer to be called the Church of Jesus Christ of Latter-day Saints (LDS). LDS began in 1830, after Joseph Smith was led to find and translate the only copy of a secret book, the Book of Mormon. This book is "the keystone of [this] religion," and people "get nearer to God by abiding by its precepts, than by any other book." LDS say they're Christian, believe in the Trinity, and revere the Bible. But that's only the King James Version (KJV), and they seem to revere the Book of Mormon even more. Their founder's other book, Doctrines and Covenants (D&C), is where LDS get all their divinely-given rules for living. They give away KJV Bibles and copies of the Book of Mormon, but keep D&C more private.

LDS consider the Trinity as three different beings, not just three different ways God expresses Godself. Father and Son have physical bodies. They believe everyone who's obedient to the rules will be saved, but those who are more obedient will be exalted above others in the afterlife. They will baptize someone on behalf of someone else who's dead. Marriage is for eternity, not just until death. Many folks hear "Mormon" and think "polygamy." Polygamy (one man, multiple wives) was taught as God's will and practiced. This has been forbidden in the LDS Church since 1890, though. All Mormon practices are said to be God-directed, with God giving such direction only to a select few. In the late 1800s, the U.S. outlawed polygamy. LDS fought this. Only when it became clear LDS couldn't win, God gave the LDS president a new directive to forbid polygamy. God also reversed the directive about prohibiting African-American males from the priesthood after the Civil Right Movement. LDS has no clergy, but men can become part of the priesthood, meaning they "have the authority to act in God's name." Critics have said LDS believe they'll each become gods and be given their own planet, populated with their children. This is inaccurate; it's not a "planet," but a "world," which will be populated by their "spirit children," over whom they will rule.

For more about decidedly non-Christian religions, see the Faith Out Loud lesson "Christianity vs. Other Faiths.")

THEOLOGICAL UNDERPINNINGS

It is a dangerous and arrogant thing to declare someone else as not a Christian, especially when that person or group says they are. CPs acknowledge this (Confession of Faith 5.31), but that doesn't mean we are to assume everyone who says they're Christian really is (Matthew 7:21-23). To be fair, there are people in our own churches every week who are not actually Christian; they're just there for the fellowship or prestige, but they've never fully committed their lives to God through Jesus Christ.

Any group, designated below as incompatible with CP theology is so, because they deny or contradict one or more of the following points of doctrine:

- There is one true God, a Holy Trinity (Confession of Faith 1.02)
- The Bible was inspired by God and brings us God's word (1.05, 1.07)
- Jesus Christ was "truly human and truly divine," and the Savior (3.07-3.08)
- Baptism itself doesn't save anybody (5.22)
- Obedience can't earn salvation (6.08)
- Resurrection of the body (7.03)

God does heal, and prayer is effective, but Christian Science is not compatible with Cumberland Presbyterianism. Jesus is more than an example; he is Savior.

Jesus was fully divine and fully human. God is triune. So, Jehovah's Witness' theology is not compatible with Cumberland Presbyterianism.

Though some of their practices seem strange to us, Seventh Day Adventist theology is mostly compatible with Cumberland Presbyterianism. Sunday worship developed as a way to honor Jesus' resurrection, which happened on a Sunday.

Although LDS theology is confusing, complicated, and apparently partially hidden from outsiders, from what we know, we can say it's not compatible with Cumberland Presbyterianism. No baptism is performed on behalf of the dead. LDS is works-oriented, linking salvation with behaviors. It's also reward-focused, as if heaven is all about us being rewarded for our obedience while on earth. Plus, secret knowledge given by God to one person is always suspect. That's why CPs discern God's will in community.

APPLYING THE LESSON TO YOUR OWN LIFE

In your congregation (or in your previous congregations, if applicable), what have you been taught about the groups mentioned in this lesson? What have you learned about them from other sources? Check around to learn how many of the groups mentioned in this lesson have churches/buildings in your area. Could your congregation benefit from a series of studies on groups such as these? If so, ask your session to consider it.

How do you act when the Jehovah's Witnesses or the Mormons knock on your door?
Where does politeness end and Christian hospitality begin? Where does Christian hospitality end and defending the faith begin? Where does defending the faith end and sharing the gospel begin?

Have you ever met someone from another faith, and realized that they are a more devout (fill in the blank with their faith) than you are a Christian?

As a Christian and Cumberland Presbyterian, what's your duty to persons within other faiths? Answer first, then check Confession of Faith 5.30.

Does Matthew 7:1-2 affect this lesson? If so, how? If not, why not?

Consider finding somewhere you can attend a Seder meal. ("Seder" = "order" it's the ritual surrounding the Passover meal.) This would not be a regular Jewish Seder, but one planned and prepared, so that Gentiles could be present. Many Christians find that this experience deepens their appreciation of the Lord's Supper.

DIGGING DEEPER

What we humans believe about God doesn't change God. What we believe about how God does things doesn't dictate what God does. But these beliefs do affect how we live, how we attempt to relate to God, how we act, and how we express forgiveness, mercy, grace, and Christian love. What we believe affects how we live, and that's why the whole idea of "all religions are pretty much the same" is false, and why it's important for your students to know what the Cumberland Presbyterian Church believes.

As for some of the groups mentioned in this lesson, perhaps C.S. Lewis put it best when he said, "If you are a Christian, you do not have to believe that all the other religions are simply wrong all through....You are free to think that all these religions, even the queerest ones, contain at least some hint of the truth... . But, of course, being a Christian does mean thinking that where Christianity differs from other religions, Christianity is right and they are wrong. As in arithmetic—there is only one right answer to a sum, and all the other answers are wrong; but some of the wrong answers are much nearer being right than others" (Mere Christianity Book II, Chapter 1).

JUST IN CASE

If a student needs help grasping what's wrong with the "all religions are equally valid" idea, try telling this story from Tony Campolo (recounted here from memory). Tony was in conversation with a stranger on a plane flying to Philadelphia. When the other man learned Tony was Christian, he dismissed Christianity as narrow-minded and proudly proclaimed his belief, that there are many ways to get into heaven. Later, as they were approaching the airport in Philadelphia, they ran into a terrible storm. Tony said to the other guy something like, "I'm glad the pilot doesn't apply your theology to flying." When the other guy asked what Tony meant, Tony said, "Somebody in that tower down there is telling our pilot what direction to fly in, what speed and altitude to fly at, and exactly which runway to land on so we don't crash into the ground or another plane. If our pilot used your way of thinking, he'd ignore the guy in the tower and say, 'Hey, there are many ways to get into Philadelphia.'"

THE CHURCH DOWN THE STREET:
IS THAT CHURCH DOWN THE STREET CHRISTIAN?

SCRIPTURE
MATTHEW 7:21-23, JOHN 14:6, 2 PETER 2:1-3

RESOURCES
- Faith Fact sheets

- Newsprint or dry erase board

- Markers or dry erase markers

- Faith Facts Quiz

LEADER PREP

BEFORE THE LESSON
Set up the room where you can form four groups. (If your group can not have four groups with more than 3-4 in each group, set up the room for two groups). Have all materials for this lesson ready for each group. Make sure not to give the students the Faith Fact sheets with the answers on them.

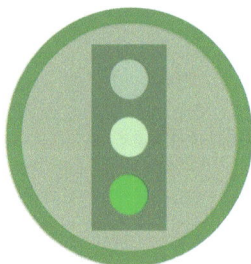

GET STARTED (15 minutes)
SAY:Today we are going to explore a few churches down the street that we aren't quite sure if they are like other Christian sects/communities. We won't be talking about religions like Islam or Judaism, but rather expressions of faith that might be considered Christian by some but not Christian by others.

GET STARTED

Pick someone to write responses to questions below on newsprint or dry erase board.

ASK: What makes someone a Christian? What things does one have to believe or do in order to be called a Christian?

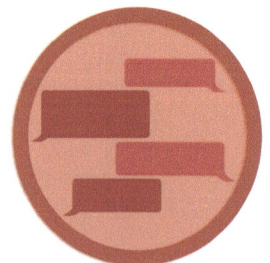

DISCUSSION QUESTIONS

LISTEN UP (25 minutes)
Break into four groups (or two), and give each group one of the Faith Fact sheets. Have each group take a few minutes to read over their Faith Fact sheet. Once each group has finished reading, have them tell the other groups about the faith group they read about. Take back the Faith Fact sheets and have them stay in groups to do the next activity.

LISTEN UP

NAME THAT GROUP

The Faith Facts Quiz has 10 faith facts about the four different religious groups that you just read about. Have each group pick one person from their group to answer the question. Once each group has chosen one person, have all four of them stand up. Ask a question from the Faith Facts Quiz. The first person to raise their hand gets one shot answering the question.

If they miss it, they are eliminated from the game and go sit on the other side of the room. The other teams get a chance to answer. If they miss it, they are eliminated from the game as well. If the first person or another person get it right, then they get to sit back with their team, and all the others are eliminated. Repeat this until each group's members have had a chance to answer by standing up, or you run out of questions.

If you do not have enough for groups, just give each person a
Faith Fact sheet to read and discuss, and then have them answer
the10 questions to see who can answer the most correctly.

DIGGING DEEPER

If you would like to share a bit more about these four faith communities with your
group, you can go online and check out more on all four using the links provided below.
http://www.religionfacts.com/compare/religions
http://www.religionfacts.com/mormonism/facts
http://www.christiansciencect.org/committee-on-publication/QuickFacts.pdf
http://www.religionfacts.com/seventh-day-adventist
http://www.religionfacts.com/jehovahs-witnesses/facts

NOW WHAT? (10 minutes)
ASK: Do any of you know someone who belongs to one of these faith communities? Have you ever spoken to them about their faith?

ASK: If you were to talk to someone that was a part of one of these faith communities, what questions would you ask them?

NOW WHAT

Take some time as a group to come up with questions you would ask someone who was Mormon, Seventh Day Adventist, Christian Scientist, and Jehovah's Witness. Write them on newsprint or on a dry erase board.

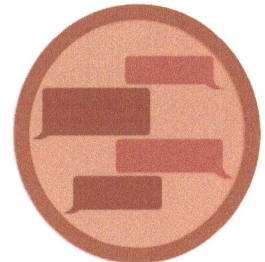

DISCUSSION QUESTIONS

After coming up with these questions,

SAY: We are not here to make fun of someone else's beliefs or to judge them on their belief. We should desire to understand why someone believes what they believe. We might not know someone who is Mormon, Seventh Day Adventist, Christian Scientist, or Jehovah's Witness. We might think that some of what they believe is different or weird. They would probably say the same about what you believe, too.

In each of these different communities of faith lies a familiarity to traditional Christian belief and variations of Christian beliefs. The same could be said about Presbyterians, Methodists, Baptists, Lutherans, Episcopalians, Catholics and so on and so forth. We should learn to understand one another, and get to know one another before passing judgment upon one another.

Having faith in God should be celebrated by all who believe in Jesus Christ. It doesn't mean we have to agree with one another, but we should at least have a respect for one another, and the beliefs we have.

If you have time, talk to someone from these faith communities, or contact someone and ask them to share with you about their beliefs. You can ask them some of the questions that were asked during the Now What? section. Share what you talked about with your group the next time you meet.

LIVE IT

LIVE IT (5 minutes)
As we close this time together, let's pray that God helps us, through Jesus Christ, to love one another—that God puts in our path someone who believes differently than us and will help us grow in our understanding of our faith.

Ask someone to close in prayer.

NOTES

Resources used in compiling background information: An Encyclopedia of Religions in the United States by William Williamson, christianscience.com, exmormon.org, Handbook of Denominations by Frank Mead, jw.org, Mere Christianity by C.S. Lewis, mormon.org, mormonnewsroom.org, Religions of America by Leo Rosten, The Book of Mormon, http://www.religionfacts.com/compare/religions, http://www.religionfacts.com/mormonism/facts, http://www.christiansciencect.org/committee-on-publication/QuickFacts.pdf, http://www.religionfacts.com/seventh-day-adventist, http://www.religionfacts.com/jehovahs-witnesses/facts. Pictures used: Sunset Down Grafton by Martin Cathrae - https://goo.gl/jCmR8q, Christian Scientists Logo - https://goo.gl/rsrKsb, Seventh Day Adventists Logo - http://goo.gl/YxyJbA, Counting the pews by Ben Garrett - https://goo.gl/ksN6AB

MORMON'S FACT SHEET

Mormons prefer to be called the Church of Jesus Christ of Latter-day Saints (LDS). LDS began in 1830, after Joseph Smith was led to find and translate the only copy of a secret book, the Book of Mormon. This book is "the keystone of [this] religion" and people "get nearer to God by abiding by its precepts, than by any other book."

LDS say they're Christian, believe in the Trinity, and revere the Bible. But that's only the King James Version(KJV), and they seem to revere the Book of Mormon even more. Their founder's other book, Doctrines and Covenants (D&C), is where LDS get all their divinely-given rules for living. They give away KJV Bibles and copies of the Book of Mormon, but keep D&C more private.

LDS consider the Trinity as three different beings, not just three different ways God expresses Godself. Father and Son have physical bodies. They believe everyone who's obedient to the rules will be saved, but those who are more obedient will be exalted above others in the afterlife. They will baptize someone on behalf of someone else who's dead. Marriage is for eternity, not just until death.

Many folks hear "Mormon" and think "polygamy." Polygamy (one man, multiple wives) was taught as God's will and practiced. This has been forbidden in the LDS Church since 1890, though. All Mormon practices are said to be God-directed, with God giving such direction only to a select few. In the late 1800s, the U.S. outlawed polygamy. LDS fought this. Only when it became clear LDS couldn't win, God gave the LDS president a new directive to forbid polygamy. God also reversed the directive about prohibiting African-American males from the priesthood after the Civil Rights Movement. LDS has no clergy, but men can become part of the priesthood, meaning they "have the authority to act in God's name."

JEHOVAH'S WITNESSES FACT SHEET

Jehovah's Witnesses say they're Christian, because they follow the teachings of Jesus Christ, whom they believe is the key to salvation, and in whose name persons are baptized and prayers are offered. But they don't think Jesus was God incarnate. He was a human who lived in perfect obedience to God, and who now rules God's heavenly kingdom. They deny the Trinity, and believe they're the only true religion.

Critics deride this group's claim (drawn from Revelation 7:4-8) that only 144,000 people will be saved. The actual teaching, however, is that 144,000 will be "co-rulers" with Jesus in Heaven; all other humans who "prove themselves obedient to God" will live on a perfected Earth after the resurrection. Those not worthy simply cease to exist, as there is no place of eternal punishment.

Jehovah's Witnesses support everything they believe with scripture. They emphasize moral living and have a strong emphasis on sharing their faith with others.

SEVENTH DAY ADVENTIST FACT SHEET

Seventh Day Adventists believe the Bible teaches 28 "Fundamental Doctrines"; the Bible was inspired by God; God is triune; Jesus was God incarnate, fully human and fully divine, and died for our sins; it is through him alone that we are saved. They focus a lot on the end times and have specific beliefs about what happens after death.

Adventists believe the end of the world and Christ's second coming are near, and it's their duty to warn everyone, but they've never set a specific date. Saturday, the Sabbath, is their holy day, because the Bible says so. They practice foot washing, because Jesus said to (John 13:14).

CHRISTIAN SCIENTIST FACT SHEET

Christian Scientists are members of the Church of Christ, Science, best known for relying on prayer rather than medicine. True healing, they say, comes from God. Refusing medicine is not required of members; they're officially free to make their own decisions about healthcare. Everything seems centered on healing for them, probably because the founder started this movement after being healed from injuries sustained in a fall. Her followers seem to hold her writings as equally important as the Bible.

This group acknowledges one God, Christ, the Holy Spirit, that humankind is made in God's image, and that humankind is saved through Christ. But they say Jesus' crucifixion and resurrection "uplift faith to understand eternal Life," not that these events atoned for our sins. All their talk of Jesus is about him as an example to follow, not as a savior to accept.

This group believes disease and material things are unreal delusions; only spiritual things really exist and matter. Christianity teaches that God created the material world, and that each human is equally mind, body, and spirit; without any one of which we're not human, which is why we believe in the resurrection of the body after death. Christianity also teaches self-sacrifice for the common good, but this group seems overly focused on what God can do for the individual.

FAITH FACTS QUIZ
ANSWER SHEET

1. This faith community believes in the power of prayer to heal a person rather than relying on medicine. (Christian Scientists)

2. This faith community teaches only 144,000 will be co-rulers with Jesus in Heaven. (Jehovah's Witnesses)

3. This faith community chooses to worship on Saturday. (Seventh Day Adventists)

4. This faith community is sometimes known as the Church of Jesus Christ of Latter-day Saints. (Mormons)

5. This faith community believes in God and Jesus but deny the Trinity. (Jehovah's Witnesses)

6. This faith community believes disease and material things are delusions. (Christian Scientists)

7. This faith community believes the end of the world and second coming of Christ is near. (Seventh Day Adventists)

8. This faith community was founded by Joseph Smith. (Mormons)

9. This faith community reads from a sacred book, called the Book of Mormon. (Mormons)

10. This faith community teaches 28 Fundamental Doctrines. (Seventh Day Adventists)

ABOUT THE AUTHORS

Andy McClung, a lifelong Cumberland Presbyterian, was ordained to the ministry of word and sacrament in 1995. He earned an M.Div. and D.Min. from Memphis Theological Seminary and has served churches in Alabama, Mississippi, Tennessee, and Arkansas. He now enjoys serving the CP Church on the presbytery, synod, and denominational levels. Andy lives in Memphis, Tennessee with his wife (also a CP minister) and their two children.

Joanna Simmerman works as the Youth & Children's Director at the Bowling Green Cumberland Presbyterian Church in Kentucky. She grew up in the United Methodist tradition. She graduated from the Center for Youth Ministry Training and from Memphis Theological Seminary in 2013 with a Master of Arts in Youth Ministry. She loves superheroes, alpacas, books, snow, and bouncy balls.

Jamie Adams has been a CP since utero. She worked with youth and children since 1997. She has directed church camps and mission trips for the west tennessee presbytery. She has served on discipleship Ministry Team since 2010. She has worked for six years as youth pastor at Union City Cumberland Presbyterian Church. Jamie recently started as pulpit supply at Cool Springs CPC and she is Technology Director of Lake County Schools. In her spare time she repairs cell phones. She has been married for 21 years to her husband, Jason. And Jason and Jamie have to of their own CP youth - Matthew and Audrey.

Rev. Nathan Wheeler is the coordinator of youth and young adult ministries for the Cumberland Presbyterian Church and serves as part of the Discipleship Ministry Team. Nathan lives in Memphis, Tennessee with his wife Marissa, their cat Spirit and their dog Lucky. He has served as a youth minister or young adult minister for over 12 years in the CPC, PCUSA and United Methodist Churches. Nathan graduated from Bethel University with a B.S. in psychology and an M.Div. from Memphis Theological Seminary.